THE HOUSES WERE STILL FULL OF SMOKE

Leonel Rugama

Azul Editions
2005

Limited Edition Copyright © 2005 Azul Editions
© 1984 Editorial Nueva Nicaragua, 3rd edition
Translation Copyright © 1985, 2005 Sara Miles,
Richard Schaaf, Nancy Weisberg
All Rights Reserved

These translations were first published
under the title
The Earth Is A Satellite Of The Moon,
Curbstone Press, 1985.

This limited first edition
is published by
Azul Editions
USA

ISBN: 1-885214-27-8

Azul Editions
www.Azuleditions.com

CONTENTS

EPITAFIO   8

EPITAPH   9

LA TIERRA ES UN SATÉLITE DE LA LUNA   10

THE EARTH IS A SATELLITE OF THE MOON   11

O TO PLAY CHESS   14

GAMES   20

ENDING UP ALL SCREWED UP   26

THE BOOK OF "CHÉ"   30

BIOGRAPHY   33

THE HOUSES WERE STILL FULL OF SMOKE   34

RAMPS AND RAMPS AND RAMPS   36

THE BASKETS ARE EMPTY   39

THE JOURNEY OUT . . .   40

UNDER THE SCORCHING SUN   45

PARA QUE SE DEN CUENTA 50

SO YOU'LL KNOW 51

COMO LOS SANTOS 52

LIKE THE SAINTS 53

EPITAFIO 74

EPITAPH 75

AFTERWORD 77

THE HOUSES WERE STILL FULL OF SMOKE

EPITAFIO

Leonel Rugama
gozó de la tierra prometida
en el mes más crudo de la siembra
sin más alternativa que la lucha,
muy cerca de la muerte,
pero no del final.

—1970

EPITAPH

Leonel Rugama
rejoiced in the promised land
in the hardest month of the planting
with no choice but the struggle
very near death
but nowhere near
the end.

—1970

LA TIERRA ES UN SATÉLITE DE LA LUNA

El Apolo 2 costó más que el Apolo 1
el Apolo 1 costó bastante.

El Apolo 3 costó más que el Apolo 2
el Apolo 2 costó más que el Apolo 1
el Apolo 1 costó bastante.

El Apolo 4 costó más que el Apolo 3
el Apolo 3 costó más que el Apolo 2
el Apolo 2 costó más que el Apolo 1
el Apolo 1 costó bastante.

El Apolo 8 costó un montón, pero no se sintió
porque los astronautas eran protestantes
y desde la luna leyeron la Biblia,
maravillando y alegrando a todos los cristianos
y a la venida el papa Paulo VI les dio la bendición.

El Apolo 9 costó más que todos juntos
junto con el Apolo 1 que costó bastante.

Los bisabuelos de la gente de Acahualinca tenían menos
 hambre que los abuelos.
Los bisabuelos se murieron de hambre.
Los abuelos de la gente de Acahualinca tenían menos
 hambre que los padres.
Los abuelos muieron de hambre.
Los padres de la gente de Acahualinca tenían menos
 hambre que los hijos de la gente de allí.
Los padres se murieron de hambre.

THE EARTH IS A SATELLITE OF THE MOON

Apollo 2 cost more than Apollo 1
Apollo 1 cost plenty.

Apollo 3 cost more than Apollo 2
Apollo 2 cost more than Apollo 1
Apollo 1 cost plenty.

Apollo 4 cost more than Apollo 3
Apollo 3 cost more than Apollo 2
Apollo 2 cost more than Apollo 1
Apollo 1 cost plenty.

Apollo 8 cost a fortune, but no one minded
because the astronauts were Protestant
they read the Bible from the moon
astounding and delighting every Christian
and on their return Pope Paul VI gave them his blessing.

Apollo 9 cost more than all the rest put together
including Apollo 1 which cost plenty.

The great-grandparents of the people of Acahualinca were
    less hungry than the grandparents.
The great grandparents died of hunger.
The grandparents of the people of Acahualinca were less
    hungry than the parents.
The grandparents died of hunger.
The parents of the people of Acahualinca were less
    hungry than the children of the people there.
The parents died of hunger.

La gente de Acahualinca tiene menos hambre que los hijos
 de la gente de allí.
Los hijos de la gente de Acahualinca no nacen por hambre,
 y tienen hambre de nacer, para morirse de hambre.
Bienaventurados los pobres porque de ellos será la luna.

The people of Acahualinca are less hungry than the
    children of the people there.
The children of the people of Acahualinca, because of
    hunger, are not born
they hunger to be born, only to die of hunger.
Blessed are the poor for they shall inherit the moon.

Acahualinca: one of the many poor barrios in Managua.

O TO PLAY CHESS

1.

Early in 1968
when I hadn't turned nineteen yet
I started playing chess
every afternoon at Carlitos Argeñal's house
playing all afternoon
    and when I'd leave
I'd leave numb from thinking so much
    and he would ask me
if I was going to come back tomorrow
    and I'd say yes
    I would always say yes
except Saturdays
because his sister went to have to hair done
and it was his turn to look after the store
    and also not on Sundays
because his sister had to get herself ready
    in the morning
to go to ten o'clock Mass
    and in the afternoon
to go to the movies.

2.

When we played he used to beat me
        and beat me
        and beat me
until I'd leave numb
but he always said

     I had potential
that he beat me with his experience
that when he'd first started
     they always beat him
        and beat him
          and *that* was worse
because after don Milcíades beat him
      he'd rub it in
and tell him he was never going to win.
We spent months playing
    in his house
on a small chessboard
where we set up some enormous pieces from a different chess set
and Carlitos would always say
     that the chessboard to those pieces
was a table and all
     that it was one of the best
because the squares instead of being painted on
    were inlaid
    (and that was better)
but that we weren't playing on it
    because it was covered
with a whole bunch of stuff
    odds & ends from the store
so it was better to play on this small chessboard.

3.

One day he received a letter
    from the chess club in Masaya
they said that they were now organized
that they had addressed the letter to him
      considering him
the most enthusiastic player in the region.

Then we began to organize
we went to get some tables
                      from a club which had broken up
but we only got one
              and it was all greasy
                      and it squeaked
and its edges were all chewed up
and Carlitos said:
"it looks like they used to crack marbles on it"
                  we found a house
and there we started playing every afternoon
and there don Constantino
                  and Fermin and Moncho came
but mostly
don Constantino, Carlitos, and me
and there we spent every afternoon playing.

4.

King's pawn to king four (KP4K)
King's pawn to king four (KP4K)
King's bishop to bishop four (KB4B)
Queen's knight to bishop three (QB3B)
        (protecting his center pawn)
Queen's knight to bishop three (QB3B)
        (protecting his center pawn)
King's bishop to bishop four (KB4B)
      (developing)
King's knight to bishop three (KK3B)
        (attacking center pawn defended by the knight)
the opening always went quickly
in silence
then it would begin:

                        hit him hit him hit him till he's exposed
when you made a good move
                        Carlitos would take his piece
                        and slowly move it
making a better one
                saying
"here no liberties will be permitted"
                                        you swallow it
                                        or you bleed to death
and check
        check
                check
friend, here you paid for a mistake with blood
friend, here you paid for a mistake with blood
friend, here you paid for a mistake with blood
friend, here you paid for a mistake with blood
                                he kept repeating it
                                and repeating it
meanwhile thinking out the series of moves
                                and in a little while
Knight to queen seven (K7Q)
                        and I kept saying
goood, gooood, goooood, goood
goood, goood, gooooooood, gooooooooood
uh-huh?
and moving and moving and moving
my leg
        as if it were trembling
                        and my shoe as if it were screeching
goooo, gooooood, goooooo, goooooooooood
                        and my shoe as if it were screeching
while he was thinking of a response.

17

O
don Tino
uh-huh Carlitos? uh Carlitos
uh-huh
Carlitos (cough coughcoughcough)
t-w-i-s-t it in
                uh-huh?
and then he moved
            then
check
you're in check
check, knight to king's bishop six (+K6KB)
you're in check (don Tinito)
you see my knights fight back hard
                              and at last
check
    check
        check
checkmate (++).

5.

Carlitos almost never lost
but the few times we beat him
        he would leave, beside himself
saying he wasn't sharp
        or wasn't feeling so good
        or hadn't eaten any lunch
he'd be going on about the great Russian champions
who even brought their wives
so their thoughts wouldn't wander off
he was saying chess was a delicate game
        if you weren't sharp, you lost.

6.

A girl always walked by the club
(but always across the street)
the same girl I'd dedicated several poems to
the one who left me "dazed in class looking at her legs"
       (from another poem)
and every afternoon she walked by from class
      and I'd be in the club playing
      or watching
and one time she told me
     she always walked by
and that I paid no attention to her.
After that, I looked for her
     and I stopped going to the club
I quit chess
("if you weren't sharp, you lost")
just like I quit soccer for chess.
By then I was nineteen
going on twenty.

GAMES

There were always kids playing over there.
In April, May and June
they used to play marbles
                shooting marbles
                    or doing tricks with marbles.
As many as forty played
in big circles
        arranging their marbles
                reds
                  yellows
                    greens
reddish-yellows and greens
yellowish-green reds
clear ones, dark ones, mediums
                olives
                    sea-greens
                      heavenly blues
The mark was pretty far
        and before shooting
they kept flicking their index finger
between the thumb and the middle finger
to steady their wrist.
        The sun like an immense yellow marble
        fell burning into the circle of the horizon.
All afternoon long:
        blowing on marbles
        winning marbles
        losing marbles
        buying marbles
        selling marbles

                jiggling marbles
                breaking marbles
We figured it was well worth the whip
                        but not the machete tip
                              nor the rack
to stay to see if the killer whale marble would bite the dust.
Maneuvering around in the dirt
spitting on our fingers
                    rubbing the marble
                    getting ready to shoot
we formed a circle
            all together
                close together
                      on top of each other
shooting the mark.
We were becoming tough guys
far away from the cars
            and trucks
                of don Aníbal.
Guarding marbles
arguing over marbles
snatching away marbles
crying over marbles.
            Until they lit the streetlamps
            and we'd go home
            I'd go in scared
            with the cold tortillas.
Valencia 50
        Montecarlo 20
                Sphinx 100
                        Polar 1000
(all over Nicaragua the foreigners are worth 1000)
or on any sidewalk.

                We played knucklebones on streetcorners
                all of June
                        August
                            and September.
Picking up knucklebones
                throwing down knucklebones
                        picking up knucklebones . . .
Dogs would pass, pissing on lampposts.
People appeared
            disappeared
            talking about work
            asking the time
                laughing
                    chatting
                        getting lost
                              turning corners.
One dignified looking gent went by on his horse
it kicked up
clattered its hooves
raised its tail
leaving behind a trail of
                    foul
                        damp
                            steaming horseshit.
Sitting on the sidewalk
              hoping for flats
                      but only turning up knucks
we were cleaned out.
Flats, flats, flats
              it made us feel like fighting
(with knucks you won, with flats you lost)
with *pininas*
        or Panamanians you won double.

In my house the knucklebones always landed
                              flats
along with the cold tortillas.
Toward October and November
blustering winds were blowing
bits of straw and dirt all over the place
                    and folks were saying it was the devil
                    and crossing themselves with ashes.
The boys flew owl-kites
                and always I'd hang around watching them
they were so far off
                turkey-buzzards would circle around them.
Some kids let out five spools of kitestring.
Our gang used to fly kites in the square
where it was always blowing up a storm
tugging the twine almost to our eyes
                        and letting it go
                    tugging it almost to our eyes
                        then letting it go . . .
the kites swayed gently side to side
                each time giving way more and more . . .
Everyone was backstepping
              backstepping
amidst the swirling gusts and the dirt
we looked like Bolívar crossing the Andes
like in the movies
                or in the storybooks.
Around this time also the circus came
with horses and monkeys
                    dogs
                      and
                        goats
and some girls that I liked

23

because at night they came out almost naked in the circus.
A bunch of us kids got together
to watch the men putting up the tents
asking them if they came from Honduras
and if they were going to give a show tonight
                                   and how much would it cost
later on we threw stones at the animals
                                   and hung from the tentpoles
until the bosses came and chased us away.
And I'd arrive in high spirits talking about the circus
                                   in my always solemn house
and get yelled at for the ice-cold tortillas.
In December
the bar owners
built fair-booths in the square
                           and covered the grounds with sawdust.
Whores from all over Nicaragua showed up
                                peddlers from Managua
                                    crap shooters
                                        con artists
big time roulette players and small fry.
They made a pit
that gave off the ornery stench of human shit
and a little bullfighting ring
                           full of oxhair and cowshit
(the peddlers from Managua were shitting in the pit)
and at night the women who sell hot punch
set themselves up across from the pit
"The earthen jar on the coals
                          the woman wrapped up in the towel"
blowing on the coals under the earthen jar
                                   (EdwinYllescas).
In the afternoon when I went by the square

to get tortillas from doña Foncha
I'd hang around in the square playing
and there I'd run into Uncle Heriberto
     who was always going around drunk
     and one time they threw him in jail
because he was yelling: VIVA AGUADO.
They put him to work uprooting brambles in the park
and my grandmother went to talk with the captain of the
               Guard
"Give him a rifle so he can go to the mountains,"
the captain told her.
And my grandmother told him that her son didn't have
criminal instincts
and if he did have them
he'd already have joined the National Guard.
I played craps
with big red dice with little black dots.
Sometimes the con artist played with us
     throwing the dice spinning them hard
     shooting the works
but he would never play roulette because they robbed you
             blind.
Until they came from home
     looking for me and for the tortillas.

         — 1968/1969

ENDING UP ALL SCREWED UP

My uncle was from a good family
but more than his stature
I remember his Costa Rican boots
                        Elegantly tapered
shining with the lustre of old ceramic tile
except for the cracks filled with dust.
                        They fastened in the back
with beautiful
          antique
          gilded
          dark
          bronze buckles.
I never saw his bare feet
but I'm sure they were pale
                  porous pale
full of bulging (not blue) veins
          and with long yellowish toenails
          covered with hairline cracks
smelling of musty cloth.
His long
    bluejeans
weren't the cleanest
    they always seemed covered with dust — but evenly —
which made a marvelous contrast to any cloudy day!
Along with his habit
                of taking too many aspirins
                he would put on a visor
whenever the sun came shining
through the doorway into the hall
while he soaked it up.

A tan visor
with green plastic
        all greasy
        and stained with sweat
                dirt
                      and age.
He used to eat with a silver fork
on a china plate
        like in the old days.
And as soon as it got dark
        he would start to pace
                back and forth
                in the living room.
Later, he would go down to the pool hall
to watch
        or play billiards
                or pool
                      or whatever.
And before coming home
he would have a strong drink
and leave, sucking on a bitter orange half.
Before falling asleep he read
        until all hours of the night
by only a single lightbulb
        (though he knew it was bad for his eyes
        and gave him a headache besides).
He read the *Digest*
        and war novels
with guys on the cover flying dive-bombers
or adventure stories like:
LOST IN THE HIGH JUNGLES OF BORNEO
illustrated with pictures of gorillas abducting women.

When I would go with the oil-lamp
                    to pee in the courtyard
                    before going to bed
he'd be reading
            and on the way back
            I'd wish him goodnight
and he'd just go on wrapped up in his reading.
There were times my grandmother got up at midnight
            because of cramps
            or some other necessity
            or to chase the cats away
            so they wouldn't knock the gourds around
and she'd check to see if my uncle was still reading.
            And he kept on taking too many aspirins.
            And he went on reading into all hours
                        of the morning.
He was a rebel
            and disrespectful
and
grandmother said he was going to end up all screwed up.
He sported a thick
            coffee-colored beard
                        peppered with grey.
He had a high forehead
            a hooked nose
and soft white hair
that was always slicked back.

Just now I came across
that book
        on the shelf
LOST IN THE HIGH JUNGLES OF BORNEO
the pages are almost falling out

and the cover is missing.
It reminds me of when my uncle
got lost:
   He wasn't in his bed
and the kitchen door was left wide open.
That day they got me up early
to search the whole house for him.
I even peeked down
      the well
         and down the shit-hole
and was looking all over the courtyard.
I had to listen to what all the neighbors were saying
as they gathered, very upset, over the disappearance.
Also I had to go down the street with a plate
to buy some rolls
     telling my friends
     that my uncle was lost
that I wasn't going to class
that I might just go to school
     to get the teacher's permission
to look for my lost uncle.
All the kids laughed at me
saying my uncle wasn't some little kid to get lost like that.

All over again
I see the gorillas who abduct women.

THE BOOK OF "CHE"

The book of "Che"
son of Augusto
son of Lautaro:
Lautaro
      "Inche Lautaro
      apubim ta pu huican"
      (I am Lautaro who finished off the Spaniards)
married to Guaconda
and brother, in turn, of Caupolicán (the celestial archer)
and of Colocolo,
Lautaro begat Oropello;
Oropello begat Lecolón
and his brothers;
Lecolón begat Cayeguano;
Cayeguano begat Talco;
Talco begat Rengo;
Rengo begat Túpac-Amaru;
Túpac-Amaru begat Túpac-Yupanqui;
Túpac-Yupanqui begat Tucapel;
Tucapel begat Urraca of Panama;
Urraca begat Diriangén of Nicaragua
and the latter committed suicide
on the slopes of the Casitas volcano
so he would never be captured.
Diriangén begat Adiact
and the latter was hanged
from a tamarind branch that is in Subtiaba.
"Here died the last Indian chief"
and folks from all over come to see it as a great thing
Adiact begat Xochitl Acatl (Cane Flower)

Xochitl Acatl begat Guegue Miquistl (Old Dog)
Guegue Miquistl begat Lempira;
Lempira begat Tecún-Umán;
Tecún-Umán begat Moctezuma Lluicámina;
Moctezuma Lluicámina begat Moctezuma Zocoyotlzin;
Moctezuma Zocoyotlzin begat Cuauhtémoc;
Cuauhtémoc begat Cuauhtemotzin
and the latter was hanged by Cortés' men
and he said:
>"So I learned
>what it means to believe
>your false promises
>oh Malinche! (Cortés)
>I knew from the moment
>I did not take my life
>with my own hand
>when you entered my city
>of Tenochtitlan
>that this was the fate
>you had in store for me."

Cuauhtemotzin begat Quaupopoca;
Quaupopoca begat Tlacopán;
Tlacopán begat Huáscar;
Huáscar begat Geronimo;
Geronimo begat Gray Feather;
Gray Feather begat Crazy Horse;
Crazy Horse begat Sitting Bull;
Sitting Bull begat Bolívar;
Bolívar begat Sucre;
Sucre begat José de San Martín;
José de San Martín begat José Dolores Estrada;
José Dolores Estrada begat José Martí;

José Martí begat Joaquín Murrieta;
Joaquín Murrieta begat Javier Mina;
Javier Mina begat Emiliano Zapata;
Emiliano Zapata begat Pancho Villa;
Pancho Villa begat Guerrero;
Guerrero begat Ortiz;
Ortiz begat Sandino;
Augusto César Sandino
brother of Juan Gregorio Colindres
    and of Miguel Angel Ortez
    and of Juan Umanzor
    and of Francisco Estrada
    and of Sócrates Sandino
    and of Ramón Raudales
    and of Rufus Marín
and when he spoke he said:
    "Our cause will triumph
    because it is the cause of justice
    because it is the cause of love."
and at other times he said:
    "I will die
    with the few who are with me
    we will die as rebels
    not live as slaves."
Sandino begat Bayo;
husband of Adelita
to whom was born "CHE"
who is called Ernesto.

        —1968/69

BIOGRAPHY

His name was never written
on the old walls of the school john.
When he left the classroom for good
nobody noticed he was gone.
The sirens of the world kept silent,
never detecting his blood on fire.
His fiery intensity
became more and more unbearable,
until the shadow of the mountains
embraced the sound of his footsteps.
That virgin land nurtured him with its mystery.
Each breeze cleansed his ideal
and left him like a child, naked and white
trembling, newly bathed.
The whole world was deaf, and where
the battle began to be born
no one listened.

—1969

THE HOUSES WERE STILL FULL OF SMOKE

Ay, my country,
the colonels who piss on your walls
we have to yank them out by the roots
hang them from a tree of bitter dew
violent with the rage of the people.
                     — Otto René Castillo

To the Sandinista heroes:
    Julio Buitrago Urroz
    Alesio Blandón Juárez
    Marco Antonio Rivera Berríos
    Aníbal Castrillo Palma

I saw the holes the Sherman tank
    blew through the house in Frixone.
        And later I went to see more holes
        in another house near Santo Domingo.
And where there weren't holes from the Sherman
    there were holes from Garand rifles
        or from Madzens
        or Brownings
or from who knows what.
The houses were still full of smoke
    and after two hours
        General Genie, without a bullhorn, was shouting
        they should surrender.
And before, for about two hours
and before that, for about four hours
and for about an hour

   he was shouting
              shouting
                      and he's shouting
Surrender!
Meanwhile, the tank,
                    its orders.
The Brownings
          the Madzens
                   the M-3's
                           the M-1's
and the police wagons
the grenades
            the tear-gas canisters . . .
and the Guardsmen shaking in their boots.

NOBODY EVER ANSWERED
Because the heroes never said
            they would die for their country,
they just died.

                     —1969

RAMPS AND RAMPS AND RAMPS

Her,
the one who I've hated so many times,
why doesn't she come now to satisfy
this pure desire I have to die?
      — Ernesto Gutiérrez

And large houses whose eaves almost meet.
Making caves out of the streets.
High sidewalks,
    higher doors
       and above the doors, recesses
       (flowers, leaves, caves)
that swallow up light for the houses.
From deep within the houses
transistor radios blaring
with the voices of some soap-opera
        or the news
        or songs,
or peaceful silences
among the heavy benches
and beach chairs
    with faded backs
their armrests smeared with grease and dirt
their shiny seats all greasy too.

The folding screen plastered with pieces of
Cemento Canal sacks
torn pages of *La Prensa*
pages from picture books
from *Life*

movie posters.
And the curtain in the middle blowing
                                    in and then outside
now and then giving a glimpse
of the room inside
the hanging blankets
                    the old shoes
                                the chamber-pots
                                            turned
upside down.

In the street
the swirling dust shines in the sun
                    folks pass by, their backs drenched.
Polished shoes coated
with a film of dust
with underneath
            a brilliance.

On the streetcorners eternal faucets
pack down the dust
                and the girl watching where the water falls
                soaking the spots where it's still bone dry.

Ramps and ramps and ramps
and train tracks in the swirling dust.
Towards the West the barrio keeps on changing
until it comes to Calvary Church
                            and a volleyball court
where on Saturday, September 21, 1956
Rigoberto López Pérez
            played until six in the evening
and when he left

                    wiping his face with a handkerchief
and the girls tried to convince him
to keep on playing,
                    he said:
"I have to go do something."

                                        —1969

Rigoberto López Pérez: 21-year old Nicaraguan poet,
assassinated dictator Anastasio Somoza Debayle on Sept. 21, 1956,
and was killed immediately by the National Guard.

THE BASKETS ARE EMPTY

The baskets are empty
waiting for food. *Life*
takes color photos of them.
The astronauts of Apollo 8
send a message of love
from the moon: "Peace on earth
to the dead of good will."

THE JOURNEY OUT...

1.

And from up on the bridge
I was watching a black man (on the boat
                                at the side of the dock)
                    who threw himself into the water
and came out with white (so white) underwear
                    stuck to his black skin.
                Who threw himself into the water
and came out
            (among the towering green waters
            with white (so white) underwear
                    stuck to his black skin
And there he was
                throwing himself
                            and throwing himself
                                    throwing himself
(from the boat
            at the side of the dock).
And I was
        watching him
                    and watching him
and I was gone (almost asleep
up on the bridge
                the longest bridge in Nicaragua
                bridge over the Siquia River).
And now I remember that that bridge
                            took so long being built
    it was something like fifty years before they finished it
    or maybe forty

      or twenty
      I don't remember how many
I just remember that one day (the day of the inauguration
                      the inauguration of the bridge
                      the longest bridge in Nicaragua
                      bridge over the Siquia River)
all the Somoza newspapers came out full of photos
and in the photos were Somoza and the bridge.
But in the movie newsreels you could see better
you saw when he (the President) cut the ribbon
and said: "This (Rte. 4) unites the Pacific Coast
          with the Atlantic"
(Rte. 4) the longest bridge in Nicaragua
         bridge over the Siquia River.

2.

The boat turned round
                    and turned
                              and turned round (on itself)
on the Siquia River
near the longest bridge in Nicaragua
until finally I didn't notice
if it had passed underneath the bridge
or had stayed behind
because when the boat began turning and turning
I was preoccupied
with the hope
that at the end of so much river-turning
it would pass under the bridge
because right there some girls were bathing
and I had seen the breasts of one of the girls

from far away
and they looked big
and I wanted to see them up close.

3.

All during the journey rock'n'roll was blasting away
while the boat glided
like a snake (slow) on the river
and a bare-legged black girl
never stopped talking
      with a black man
      in a low voice
and in English
seated forward
laughing from time to time
     talking
     in a low voice
and in English.
I took it easy, sat down, walked around
I went forward
(for the forward journey) up to where the helm was
to see the river head-on
and there I saw the tough black guy who was steering
who wasn't interested in the river
who wasn't interested in anything
who seemed like a statue
and I never found out what he was looking toward.

4.

After a great rush of waves in the bay
where the water was no longer the beautiful water of the
                                                                            river
and little by little the river had been widening out
and losing its dark green color
                      dark, transparent green
like pieces of glass from Shaler Cola bottles
                      (dark, transparent green)
and the smell of the earth softly moistening
and the trees
                    on the riverbanks dense with vegetation
the trees bending down towards the water of the river
as though they were drinking
                or were Hindus prostrate at the feet of their Raj
And losing also
            its river-water mystery
that shelters serpents
                  and lizards
its cold mystery
                  its icy pools
with their depths a tangle of fallen trees
and branches
                branches
and vines
muddy branches
                and muddy vines
and long gobs of slime hanging down
like squares of old quilts
dark areas
where you could stay bound
to all kinds of bodies in the deep.

After a great rush of waves in the bay
where the water was no longer the beautiful water of the
river
we pulled into Bluefields, and docked:
there, where heaps of garbage float on the water
and heaps of old
       wet
          pulpy turds
move as if dancing this way and that
and where the water moves pestered
by all the toad-slime
pestered and harassed
there, where there's a very old dock
with beat-up rotting planks
and on the first shack stuck to the dock
facing the bay
there's an almost life-size poster
of Somoza, smiling
and he's not the old man.

The old man: Refers to ex-President Anastasio Somoza Debayle, who established the Somoza dictatorship in 1936. After his assassination in 1956, his two sons, first Luis and then Anastasio Somoza II, ruled the country until the triumph of the Nicaraguan Revolution in 1979, led by the Sandinista National Liberation Front (FSLN).

UNDER THE SCORCHING SUN
"I was thirsty and you gave me drink."
(famous saying)

1.

And mounds of crates of empty beer bottles
and mounds
        and mounds
and mountains of mounds
             of crates of empty beer bottles . . .
giving the impression of some lost Indian civilization
giving the impression of fabulous pyramids
long suffering from the elements
          crates of empty beer bottles
            pine crates
              bleached
              dried
              parched
              burnt
              split by the sun
and their bottoms also bleached
          full of splotches of mud
            splattered with splotches of mud
              with splotches
                  and splotches
of black mud.

2.

Launches
      or sailboats
      or motorboats
tied to the dock
(like horses tied up at hitching posts)
And the puff-puff pulling up to the dock
                      slowly
                      with its puffs of smoke
                      puff-puff-puff-puff-puff-puff
                      with its puffs of smoke
                      slowly
        pulling up to the dock.
And the boat rocking gently side to side
                          and tied to the dock
and black men heaving crates of empty beer bottles
and others stacking them up on the boat
and the boat rocking gently side to side
                      and other blacks
                      and blacks
and more black men lugging
                    and lugging
crates of full beers from the boat
                down to the dock
and on the dock
        mounds
            and mounds
                  mountains of mounds
of crates of full beers.
Behind it all
      on the walls of the store
of the store that faces the bay
Somoza's big smile.

3.

The first block is packed with signs
Hong Kong
   food
     lodging
       General Store
          we buy
            we sell
Quan
  Morgan
     Chiong
       Chiang
         Campbell
           Sujo
             Hooker
               Rigby
The first block
    climbing uphill
       uphill
and the sun beating down on your face
        and the sweat
        the stink
and the sun beating down on your face
        the sun reflecting off the pavement
        the sweltering sun
and the reflection hitting you in the eyes
   the glare
   the unbearable heat
        and the sweat
the stink
the sun beating down on your face

and you
       asking for a little water
              and the water brackish.

4.

Later on, I continued walking
bearing up under the scorching sun
                        and the sweat
along the sidewalks
    but it's the same as walking in the middle of the street
because the sidewalks seem like long strips of desert
and there's no shade from the eaves
around here
       and with the sun beating down on my face
I realized
       that the stadium
       the stadium in Bluefields is named Somoza
and the sun reflecting off the hill
and the sun beating down on my face
and the sun hitting me in my eyes
       "Sun times sun times sun times sun"
and almost all day long
       a fly buzzing around under the sun
people moving around like lizards
       solitary
       under the sun
lizards under the sun
       cocks inflamed by the sun
       adobe walls baked by the sun
       yokes broken by the sun

  feathers
       hides
           ropes
              stones
splitting apart under the sun (Edwin Yllescas)
until I came to a park
where there's an old fountain
and a statue of Rigoberto Cabezas
                       or of Zelaya
or someone or other.

PARA QUE SE DEN CUENTA

> —Sí pero no tocamos
> —No se ve cuando se toca, dijimos.
> Vamos,
> sigamos viendo cuanto vimos.
> —Carlos Martínez Rivas

Hace bastante vi las piernas de una muchacha.
Como los dientes de leche eran blanquísimas,
semejantes no sé en qué al vidrio pulido
de un carro nuevo.

Me quedé ido
hasta que ella hizo el vano intento
de alargarse el vestido.

Yo continué explicando:
"para aprender matemáticas es necesario
absoluta concentración." Comencé a demostrar
el Teorema del Residuo, o el de Pitágoras
o el de Ruffini.

No resistí continuar
y al rato consideraba lo fresco, lo húmedo,
lo suave de las piernas de aquella muchacha.

Cuando me callaba, todos pensaban
que resolvía una abstracción metamática.
Pero yo veía las piernas,
casi todos los días le veía las piernas,
y nunca pude tocárselas.

—1969

SO YOU'LL KNOW

> "Yes, but don't touch."
> "You can't see when you touch," we said.
> "Come on,
> let's keep on looking, we saw so much."
> — Carlos Martínez Rivas

A while ago I saw the legs of a girl.
Like baby teeth they were pure white
resembling — I don't know — the polished windows
of a new car.

                        I was dazed
until she made a vain attempt
to pull her skirt down.

I went on explaining:
"to grasp mathematics absolute concentration
is necessary." I began to demonstrate
the Remainder Theorum, or the Pythagorean Theorum,
or Ruffini's.

I didn't stop talking
and, from time to time, I thought about the fresh, moist
softness of that girl's legs.

When I did stop, they all thought
I had solved some mathematical abstraction.
But I was looking at her legs,
just about every day I looked at her legs
and I never could touch them.

— 1969

COMO LOS SANTOS

Ahora quiero hablar con ustedes
o mejor dicho
ahora estoy hablando con ustedes.

Con vos
con vos tunco carretonero
con vos estoy hablando.

Con vos carbonero
          carbonero encontilado
  vos
  vos que llevás ese cipote
                  enganchado
                  sobre el carretón
y lo llevás sosteniendo la lata
y todo encontilado.

Vos amarraste una vez
        hace tiempo
        un trapo
        un trapo acabado de lavar
        todo ajado
        ajado y niste
y que lo amarraste en uno de los brazos del carretón
                para secarte el sudor
                  y la tierra
                  y el tilde
                  y todo revuelto
y el trapo
está mugroso

LIKE THE SAINTS

Now I want to talk with you
or rather
now I am talking with you

With you
with you, pork peddler
I'm talking with you

With you, charcoal seller
       charcoal seller covered in soot
    you
    you who carry that youngster
               hitched
                 on top of your cart
and you cart it enduring the boredom
and everything covered in soot

One time
    a while ago
    you tied up a rag
    a rag that had just been washed
    all wrinkled
    wrinkled and stained
you tied it to one of the poles of the cart
    to wipe away your sweat
    the dirt
    the censure
    the whole mess
and the rag
is filthy

y hasta echa un olor a agrio
que vos lo sentís de viaje
                cuando te secas la cara
                o el pescuezo.
    A vos te hablo
a vos que te suben el rango de la miseria
cada vez que te sale otra tira guindando del pantalón
vos que sos marca mundial
en el récord de los ayunos
¡qué cuarenta noches!
¡y qué cuarenta noches!
A vos que se te asoma
curioso el calzoncillo nacido
                por todo lo roto del pantalón
y hay gente que sale a la puerta
                y que se pone a reír
hasta que doblás la esquina
chapaleando tufo
y seguís empujando
y con las rodillas peladas
y con el pecho consumido
                y desnudo.
Con vos estoy hablando
con vos mismo
sí, sí
    a vos te digo.

Con vos también
            aseado chofer particular
            engrasado taxista
            camionero polvoso
            busero gordo
            soldador borracho

and gives off a bitter stink
that you smell as you go
      when you wipe your face
          or your neck
I'm speaking to you
to you who come up through the ranks of misery
each time with more shreds hanging from your pants
you who hold the world's record
in the record book of fasting:
what a forty days!
and what a forty nights!
To you whose underwear comes
clean through
    the complete defeat of your pants
and people come to their doorways
    who start to laugh
as you turn the corner
splattering foul-smelling
and you keep on pushing
    with your knees bare
    your naked, tubercular chest
I'm speaking with you
you yourself
yes, yes
with you
  I'm speaking

With you too
  clean private chauffeur
  greasy taxidriver
  dusty truckdriver
  fat busdriver
  drunken welder

            zapatero remendón
            judío errante afilador de cuchillos
                        de hachas
                        machetes y tijeras
con todos los vende sorbetes y raspados
y con todos los vendedores ambulantes.

Con vos también
        cipote vende chicles
        y con el otro
        el que vende bolis congelados
        y el que vende gelatinas
        y también con el de la bolsa de confites de coco
y con el de la bolsa de leche de burras
y con todos los lustradores vulgares
(aunque digan que más vulgar es mi madre)
y también háblenle a los ciegos
        a los ciegos que piden limosna en las paradas
        y a los otros ciegos de guitarras o sin guitarras
        (y a los proletarios de la música)
        y a los tullidos de toda clase
        y a los tísicos del estadio
        y a los mudos y sordos de nacimiento.

Pásenle la voz a los basucas
y diganles que vengan
llamen a los chivos sifilíticos
y a los rateros
y a los busca pleitos en las cantinas
en los estancos y en los putales
tráiganse también
a toda la mancha de vagos
a todos los vagos de todos los barrios

      shoemaker
      wandering jew sharpener of knives
                    hatchets
                      machetes and scissors
with everyone who sells sherbets and ices
and with all the street peddlers

With you too
      kid selling chiclets
      and with the other one
      the one selling frozen snowcones
      and the one selling gumdrops
      and also the one with his bag of coconut sweets
and the one with a bag of caramels
and with all the common shoeshine boys
(though they say my mother's even more common)
And also, let's talk to those who are blind
      to the blind who beg for alms at bus stops
      and to the others also blind, with guitars or without
      (to the proletarians of music)
      and to the crippled of every kind
      and to the tubercular wards of the State
      and to those deaf and dumb from birth

Let the garbage collectors know
and speak to them who come
call out the syphilitic kids
and the petty thieves
the troublemakers in the bars
in the smokeshops and whorehouses
and bring with you also
the whole motley crew of do-nothings
all those hanging around in all the barrios

        que ahorita están jugando janbol
        y si no desmoche
aunque se quede el que tenga mico doble
que se vengan todos los demás
y aunque estén esperando con dos embolones.

Que se vengan todos los que están bateando
        y los que están sirviendo
que se deshagan las apuestas
            y que vengan
y que bajen las pandillas de todos lados.

SAQUEN A TODOS LOS ESQUELETOS

a todos los esqueletos que se mueran
                en Los Cauces
                en Miralagos
                en el Valle Maldito
                en Acahualinca
                en La Fortaleza
                en El Fanguito
                en las Calles del Pecado
                en La Zona
                en La Perla
                en la colonia Alta Vista
                en la colonia López Mateos
                en La Salinera
                en Cabo Haitiano
                en La Fossette
y que traigan a sus cipotes
a sus cipotes que "no nacen por hambre
        y que tienen hambre de nacer
        para morirse de hambre"

  who right now are playing handball
  and if the game can't be cut short
though the one who has both sides covered stays
all the rest should come
though you're only two points away from winning

Come on, everyone who's hitting
    and those who are serving
drop your bets
    and come on
and the gangs should come on down from all over

BRING OUT ALL THE SKELETONS

all the skeletons who die
  in Los Cauces
  in Miralagos
  in Valle Maldito
  in Acahualinca
  in La Fortaleza
  in El Fanguito
  in Calle del Pecado
  in La Zona
  in La Perla
  in Alta Vista
  in López Mateos
  in La Salinera
  in Cabo Haitiano
  in La Fossette
and bring out your kids
your kids who "because of hunger aren't born
      but who hunger to be born
     only to die of hunger"

Que vengan todas las mujeres
    la verdulera nalgona
    y la vieja asmática del canasto
    la negra vende vigorón
    y la sombreruda vende baho
    la vende chicha helada
    y la vende cebada
    la vende naranjada
    y la lavandera con las manos blanquiscas de jabón
    las poncheras de la fiesta
    y las vende gallo pinto y carne asada
    las mondongueras
    y las nacatamaleras mantecosas
    las sirvientas
    las picheles
    las rufianas
    con todo y sus zorros
y aquella muchacha hermosa que vende pan con mantequilla
y la chavalita
        que está empezando a echar tetitas
        y que vende pasteles
y todos las cipotas que venden guineos
            naranjas
            y mandarinas
            y que por un peso dan
            una bolsa.
Que vengan también las carteristas
        las cantineras
        y las putas
        y las putas viejas y tetonas
        y las putas iniciadas
háblenle a las espiritistas
    y a las medium

All the women should come
    the fat-assed fishwife
    and the asthmatic old woman with the baskets
    the black woman selling cold drinks
    and the woman in the shade selling trinkets
    the seller of cold *chicha*
    and the seller of bait
    the woman selling orangeade
    and the laundress with her hands bleached from soap
    the barmaids at parties
    and the sellers of rice and beans and barbecue
    the ones selling dried tripe
    and the makers of greasy tamales
    the servants
    the waitresses
    the madames
    all of them and their foxes
and that beautiful girl there who's selling bread and butter
and the little kid
    who's beginning to develop breasts
    who sells pastries
and all the kids who sell bananas
                  oranges
                  tangerines
                  and give for a penny
                  a paper bag
All the pickpockets should come
    the 'B-girls'
    and the whores
    the old whores with big tits
    and the whores just starting out
Let's talk to the spiritualists
    and to the mediums

   y a las endemoniadas
   a las perseguidas por los duendes
  y por los malos espíritus
   a las hechiceras
  y a las hechizadas
   a las vende filtros
  y a las compra filtros.
Ahora que están todos aquí
   que están todos aquí reunidos
         reunidos y oyéndome,
ahora quiero hablar con ustedes
o mejor dicho
ahora estoy hablando con ustedes
quiero empezar a hacerles una plática
y quiero que todos ustedes
le platiquen
    a todos los que no vinieron
y que les platiquen en voz alta cuando estén solos,
y que les platiquen en las calles
    en las casas
    en los buses
    en los cines
    en los parques
    en las iglesias
    en los billares
    en los patios montosos
    en los barrios sin luz
    y a orilla de los cercos que se están cayendo
    y a orilla de los ríos
    sentados en las cunetas
    arrimados en las mochetas de las puertas
    y asomados por las ventanas
y en fin

> the women possessed by demons
> and those persecuted by goblins
> and by evil spirits
> and to the witches
> to the bewitched
> to those who sell love-potions
> and those who buy them

Now that you are all here
all gathered here together
                together and listening to me
now I want to speak with you
or rather
now I am speaking with you
I want to begin a discussion with you
and I want you too
to discuss it
        with everyone who didn't come
and discuss it loudly when you're alone
and discuss it in the streets
> the houses
> the buses
> the movies
> the parks
> churches
> pool halls
> crowded courtyards
> barrios with no lights
> and along the walls that are crumbling
> on the banks of the rivers
> sitting in ditches
> hunkered down in doorways
> and leaning out windows

and finally

      en todas partes
y que platiquen en voz baja
                cuando no estén solos
o mejor dicho cuando está un rico cerca
o cuando está un guardia de un rico cerca.

Yo les quería platicar
que ahora vivo en las catacumbas
y que estoy decidido a matar el hambre que nos mata
cuando platiquen esto
platíquenlo duro
cuando no esté uno de los que siembra el hambre
o un oreja de los que siembra el hambre
o un guardia de los que siembra el hambre.

Cállense todos
y síganme oyendo
      en las catacumbas
      ya en la tarde cuando hay poco trabajo
      pinto en las paredes
      en las paredes de las catacumbas
      las imágenes de los santos
      de los santos que han muerto matando el hambre
      y en la mañana imito a los santos.
Ahora quiero hablarles de los santos.

SANDINO

"Había un nica de Niquinohomo
que no era ni político
                ni soldado"

>   everywhere
> and discuss it in a low voice
>   when you are not alone
> or rather
> when there's a rich man close by
> or when there's a rich man's guard close by

I would like to discuss with you
how now I live in the catacombs
and how determined I am to kill the hunger that is killing us
when you discuss this
discuss it long and hard
when no one who sows hunger is around
nor a spy for those who sow hunger
nor a guard for those who sow hunger

Quiet, all of you
and follow me listening
    in the catacombs
        now, in the afternoons, when there's not much work
        I paint on the walls
        the walls of the catacombs
        images of the saints
        the saints who died killing hunger
        and in the morning I imitate the saints
Now I want to talk to you about the saints:

SANDINO

"There was a Nica from Niquinohomo
who was neither a politician
                    nor a soldier"

luchó en Las Segovias
y una vez que le escribió a Froylán Turcios
le decía que si los yanquis
por ironía del destino
le mataban a todos sus guerrilleros
en el corazón de ellos
encontraría el tesoro más grande de patriotismo
y que eso humillaría a la gallina
que en forma de águila
ostenta el escudo de los norteamericanos
y más adelante le decía
que por su parte al verse solo (cosa que no creía)
se pondría en el centro de cien quintales de dinamita
que tenía en su botín de guerra
y que con su propia mano daría fuego
y que dijeron a cuatrocientos kilómetros a la redonda:

SANDINO HA MUERTO.

EL "CHE"

"Ni un tanque
ni una bomba de hidrógeno
ni todas las bolitas del mundo"
lucha en todas partes
y en todas partes
florecen las higueras
del río bajan montones de guerrilleros
en Higueras del Río dicen que lo mataron
"CHE" comandante
nosotros somos el camino
y vos el caminante

He fought in Las Segovias
and one time when he wrote to Froylán Turcios
he told him that if the Yankees
by some irony of fate
killed all his guerrillas,
they would find in their hearts
the great treasure of patriotism
and that it would humiliate the chicken
who shows off like an eagle
on the North American coat of arms.
And further he said
that for his part if he found himself alone
(something he didn't believe)
he would put himself in the middle of a hundred sticks of
        dynamite
that he kept in his war-chest
and with his own hand he would ignite it
so that for four hundred kilometers around they would say:
SANDINO HAS DIED.

CHE

"Not a tank
not a hydrogen bomb
nor all the ballots in the world"
He fights everywhere
and everywhere
the *higueras* bloom
mountains of guerrillas descend on the river
in *Higueras del Río* they say they killed him
CHE, comandante,
we are the path
and you the one who walks it.

MIGUEL ANGEL ORTEZ

"Y aún hecho ya polvo
se miaban de pánico los yanquis"
al comienzo Sandino no lo quería aceptar
pero él le dijo a Sandino
que él era el capitán Ferrerita
y después del combate de Ocotal
le dio una mula blanca
y se le pegó
hasta que llegó a ser
el general del coro de ángeles
murió en Palacagüina peleando mano a mano.

JORGE NAVARRO

Fue tan valiente como para no morir de tristeza.
Hablaba en las asambleas
y una vez hizo un periódico
tenía un acordeón
pero sabía que hay un deber de cantar
y otro de morir
murió con los pies engusanados
por el lodo de Bocaycito
pero resucitó
el mismo día
y por todas los lados.

MIGUEL ANGEL ORTEZ

"And even when he was already dust
the Yankees mewed like kittens in panic"
At first Sandino didn't want him
but he told Sandino
he was Captain Ferrerita
and after the fighting in Ocotal
Sandino gave him a white mule
and he drove it
until he came to be
General of the Choir of Angels
He died in Palacagúinia, fighting hand to hand.

JORGE NAVARRO

He was so brave, so as not to die of sorrow.
He used to speak his mind at meetings
and at one time he put out a newspaper
he had an accordion
because he knew one had a duty to sing
as well as to die
he died with his feet covered with worms
in the mud of Bocaycito
but that same day
he was resurrected
everywhere.

SELIM SHIBLE

Conociste a Selim.
Sabías que una vez verguió a un agente de la seguridad
en la propia oficina de seguridad
si no sabías eso
no conociste a Selim
cuando llegó a vivir por nosotros
¡murió en la perfecta manera que nació!
pero ya desde antes
desde hacía siglos era eterno.

JACINTO BACA

Con el brazo izquierdo de mampuesta
y con el derecho disparando su pistola
sí señores
hay una patrulla de JACINTOS arpillando al enemigo
y una gran estatua
aunque rota ya su sangre
creció en una plaza de Rota.

JULIO BUITRAGO

Nunca contestó nadie
porque los héroes no dijeron
que morían por la patria
sino que murieron
en julio nació Julio
seis más nueve quince
de seis y nueve sesenta y nueve

SELIM SHIBLE

You knew Selim.
Did you know that one time he beat up a security agent
inside his own security office?
If you didn't know that
you didn't know Selim.
When he came to live through us
he died in the perfect way he was born!
But now, as for centuries before
he is eternal.

JACINTO BACA

With his left arm taking aim
and his right firing the pistol
yes gentlemen
there's a band of JACINTOS sacking the enemy
and (even though it's shattered now)
a life-size statue
that rose from his blood in the Plaza de Rota.

JULIO BUITRAGO

No one ever answered
because the heroes never said
they would die for their country
they just died.
Julio was born in July
six and nine make fifteen
on the six and nine of sixty-nine

nació matando al hambre (aunque sea antipoético)
nació peleando solo
contra trescientos
es el único que nació en el mundo
superando a Leónidas
a Leónidas el de las Termópilas

"VIAJERO VE Y DI A ESPARTA A QUE MORIMOS
POR CUMPLIR SUS SAGRADAS LEYES."

ESO ESTA EN LA CASA
DONDE NACIO JULIO
lo único que está en español
pues sí
nació sin camisa
        y cantando mientras disparaba su M-3
     nació cuando trataban de matarlo
              con guardias
              con tanques
              con aviones
     nació cuando no pudieron matarlo
        y esto cuéntenselo a todo el mundo
y esto cuéntenselo a todo el mundo
platíquenlo duro
platíquenlo duro siempre
duro siempre
con la tranca en la mano
con el machete en la mano
con la escopeta en la mano.
¡Ya platicamos!

AHORA VAMOS A VIVIR COMO LOS SANTOS.

He was born killing hunger (though it's anti-poetic)
he was born fighting alone
against three hundred
he was the only one born in the world
surpassing Leonidas
Leonidas of Thermopylae.

"TRAVELER GO AND TELL SPARTA
WE DIE FULFILLING HER SACRED LAWS"

THAT WAS IN THE HOUSE
WHERE JULIO WAS BORN
only it was in Spanish
and yes
he was born without a shirt
    and was singing while he fired his M-3
  he was born when they tried to kill him
        with the Guard
        with tanks
        with planes
  he was born when they were not able to kill him
    this story you should tell to everyone
you should tell this story to everyone
you should discuss it long and hard
you should discuss it hard forever
forever hard
with a stick in your hand
with a machete in your hand
with a shotgun in your hand
let's discuss it now!

NOW LET US LIVE LIKE THE SAINTS

EPITAFIO

Aquí yacen
los restos mortales
del que en vida
buscó sin alivio
una
a
una
tu cara
en todos
los buses urbanos.

—noviembre/diciembre de 1969

EPITAPH

Here lie
the mortal remains
of one who in life
searched without relief for
one
by
one
your face
on every
bus in the city.

—november/december 1969

AFTERWORD

Doña Candida Rugama, mother of Leonel Rugama, was interviewed in 1983 by Juan José Godoy, a North American writer, living in Estelí, Nicaragua. In the following excerpts, Candida Rugama talks about her son.

From the time he was a little boy, he was sharp, ready to answer whatever you asked him about . . . he'd have conversations with you like an adult. He was witty. A joker, as he would say. And he loved to go to the circus. He always wanted to watch the circus people working, setting up the tents, getting the animals ready. He hung around talking with them, asking them a million questions . . .

He had wanted to study civil engineering. When he finished primary school, he wanted to take math classes so he could enter the seminary. I tried to talk him out of it, because we had so little money: but he was determined and I gave in. With the few pennies we had coming in from a small pension, he'd buy books and put them in his bookbag — he loved classes, and he had a regular ritual about going to school. First he would bathe, then he'd go and study some more — he had every minute of his day planned out for what he had to do.

He passed the pre-seminary courses in San Ramón High School in León, where he met Omar Cabezas. Later, it seemed he didn't want to study. He . . . who knows what difficulties he saw there. And he told me that he was going to get his diploma here, which he did, in the Francisco Luis Espinoza High School. He graduated as the best student in his class. He began to study German, and thought about getting a scholarship so he could go study in Germany. But already he had his ideals: because according to Father Cardenal, who was in the seminary, Leonel used to visit the poorest barrios in Managua. It was seeing the poverty there, said Father Cardenal, that gave birth to Leonel's ideas of service: that was where his love for humanity came from. And from that time on he demonstrated his caring. With the kids who couldn't pay for math lessons with him, he'd give them free lessons and lend them his own books. With students poorer than he was, he wound up giving them his clothes.

But the scholarship didn't come through. When he had already been accepted, someone went to the school and denounced Leonel as a leftist, and they wouldn't give him the scholarship. So he decided to enter the University in León, but not to get a degree the way he wrote and told his father, but to work for the revolution . . . he enrolled in the University under the name of "Francisco" instead of Leonel: he said he was Leonel Rugama's brother, and that's how he was able to get in.

He became a member of the FER: the student group that did revolutionary work in the high schools and in the University. Later on, he entered the FSLN . . . They tell me that when he was in the University he used to walk around with his Bible under his arm and a stack of newspapers — so if he got caught at night, he could sleep under the papers. And people would give him, say, five *córdobas* for his FER expenses, and he'd eat with two and use the rest to buy ammunition. When a friend told Leonel that there was going to be a party and the tickets were ten *córdobas*, he answered, "No! with ten *córdobas* I can buy a box of bullets."

The entire year he was at the University he hadn't been back to Estelí. By 1970 he was in Managua with three other comrades preparing to go to the mountains with the guerrillas. They had collected provisions and plenty of weapons.

He was with Mauricio Hernández Baldizón, Roberto Núñez Dávila, and Igor Ubeda, a boy from our town. And they found out that someone had turned them in to the Guard.

The daughter of a woman whose son was also a Sandinista went to warn them, bringing them food. When she saw them she shouted, "Muchachos, here comes the Guard!" They grabbed their guns — Igor Ubeda made it out and escaped to Estelí.

The Guard surrounded the house. There were about three hundred soldiers, for the three of them left in the house. The fighting lasted from one in the afternoon until about five, with tanks and bombs and helicopters. The Chief of Security kept calling to them with a bullhorn, ordering them to surrender. Finally, Leonel answered: "Tell your mother to surrender!"

They say that was his finest poem. His last verse. A little later people heard them singing the Sandinista hymn.

The other two were killed first. Leonel was dying when one of the guardsmen came in through a hole the tanks had blasted open in the side of the house, and finished him off with a bullet. He died on January 15, 1970, before making it to his twenty-first birthday.